THOMAS CRANE PUBLIC LIBRARY

QUINCY MASS

CITY APPROPRIATION

Dinosaurs Alive!

Triceratops

and Other Horned and Armored Dinosaurs

Jinny Johnson

Illustrated by Graham Rosewarne

A+

Smart Apple Media

Published by Smart Apple Media
2140 Howard Drive West
North Mankato, MN 56003

Designed by Helen James
Edited by Mary-Jane Wilkins
Artwork by Graham Rosewarne

Copyright © 2008 Smart Apple Media.
International copyright reserved in all countries.
No part of this book may be reproduced in any form
without written permission from the publisher.

Printed in China

Library of Congress Cataloging-in-Publication Data

Johnson, Jinny.
Triceratops and other horned and armored dinosaurs / by Jinny Johnson ;
illustrated by Graham Rosewarne.
p. cm. — (Dinosaurs alive!)
Includes index.
ISBN 978-1-59920-064-4
1. Triceratops—Juvenile literature. 2. Ceratopsidae—Juvenile literature. 3.
Ornithischia—Juvenile literature. I. Rosewarne, Graham, ill. II. Title. III. Series.

QE862.O65J64 2007
567.915'8—dc22   2006102834

First Edition

9 8 7 6 5 4 3 2 1

Contents

A dinosaur's world

A dinosaur was a kind of reptile that lived millions of years ago. Dinosaurs lived long before there were people on Earth.

We know about dinosaurs because many of their bones and teeth have been discovered. Scientists called paleontologists (pay-lee-on-ta-loh-jists) learn a lot about the animals by studying these bones.

The first dinosaurs lived about 225 million years ago. They disappeared—became extinct—about 65 million years ago.

Some scientists believe that birds are a type of dinosaur, so they say there are still dinosaurs living all around us!

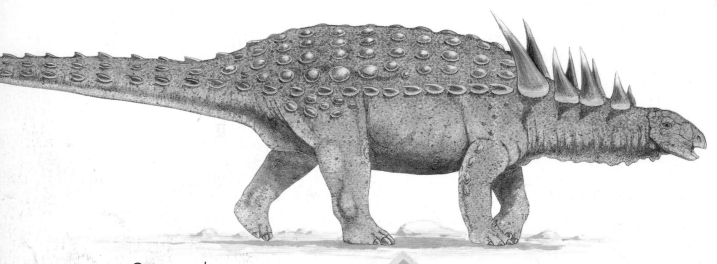

Sauropelta

TRIASSIC

248 to 205 million years ago
Some dinosaurs that lived at this time:
Coelophysis, Eoraptor, Liliensternus, Plateosaurus, Riojasaurus, Saltopus

EARLY JURASSIC

205 to 180 million years ago
Some dinosaurs that lived at this time:
Crylophosaurus, Dilophosaurus, Lesothosaurus, Massospondylus, Scelidosaurus, Scutellosaurus

LATE JURASSIC

180 to 144 million years ago
Some dinosaurs that lived at this time:
Allosaurus, Apatosaurus, Brachiosaurus, Ornitholestes, Stegosaurus, Yangchuanosaurus

Stegosaurus

EARLY CRETACEOUS

144 to 98 million years ago
Some dinosaurs that lived at this time:
Baryonyx, Giganotosaurus, Iguanodon, Leaellynasaura, Muttaburrasaurus, Nodosaurus, Sauropelta

LATE CRETACEOUS

98 to 65 million years ago
Some dinosaurs that lived at this time:
Ankylosaurus, Gallimimus, Maiasaura, Triceratops, Tyrannosaurus, Velociraptor

Tyrannosaurus

Triceratops

Imagine a huge creature that is twice the size of a rhinoceros, with an enormous horned head.

A fully grown triceratops weighed up to 11 tons (10 t)—as much as two elephants.

The triceratops had three sharp horns and a large bony frill at the back of its neck. The name triceratops means "three-horned face."

This dinosaur lived in North America. It was one of the biggest of all the horned dinosaurs.

Dinosaurs lived long before there were people on Earth. But here you can see how big a dinosaur was compared to a seven-year-old child.

The triceratops was strong enough to battle against the fiercest attackers. Even the tyrannosaurus could not always win a fight with a triceratops.

This is how you say triceratops: tri-serra-tops

TRICERATOPS

Group: horned dinosaurs (ceratopians)

Length: 29.5 feet (9 m)

Lived in: North America

When: Late Cretaceous, 67–65 million years ago

Inside a triceratops

The head of a triceratops was as long as 6.5 feet (2 m) from the tip of the nose to the back of its head—more than the length of an adult human. That is a very big head!

The triceratops had two long horns on its forehead—each about 3 feet (1 m) long. Even the little horn on its nose was 7 inches (18 cm) long.

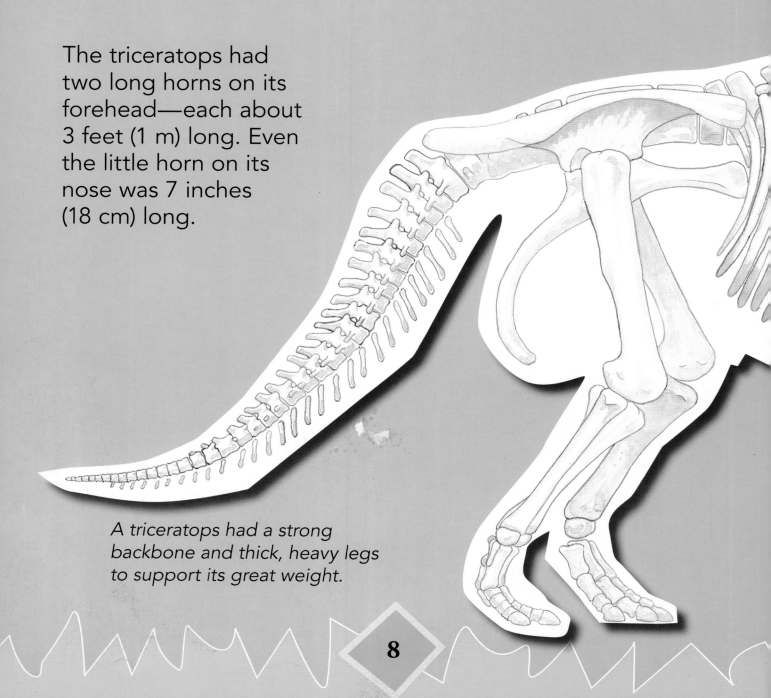

A triceratops had a strong backbone and thick, heavy legs to support its great weight.

The enormous frill at the back of this dinosaur's head was made of solid bone. It was very heavy and strong, so other creatures found it difficult to attack the triceratops.

Look at this dinosaur's jaws. It has a beak like a parrot's. This strong, sharp beak helped the dinosaur chop off mouthfuls of tough plants.

A triceratops in action

The triceratops lived in large groups called herds. Together the animals wandered slowly through the forests, feeding on plants.

The triceratops may look fierce, but it preferred to stay out of trouble. Few other dinosaurs dared to attack such a large, well-armored animal.

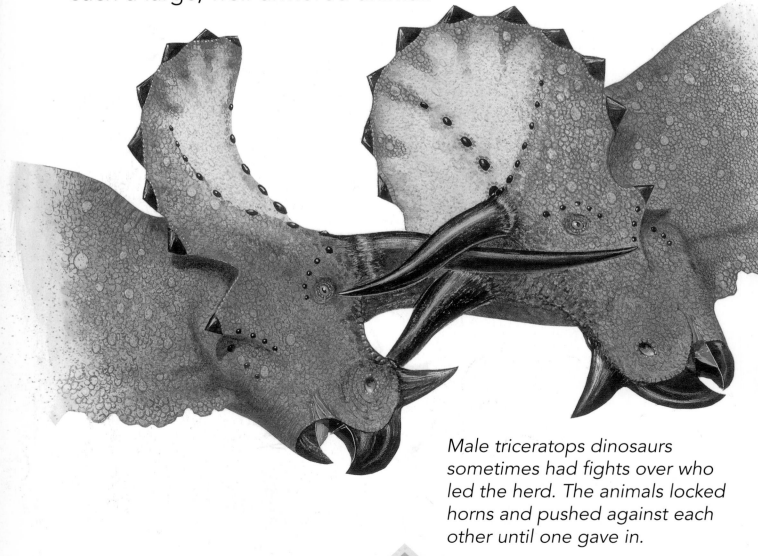

Male triceratops dinosaurs sometimes had fights over who led the herd. The animals locked horns and pushed against each other until one gave in.

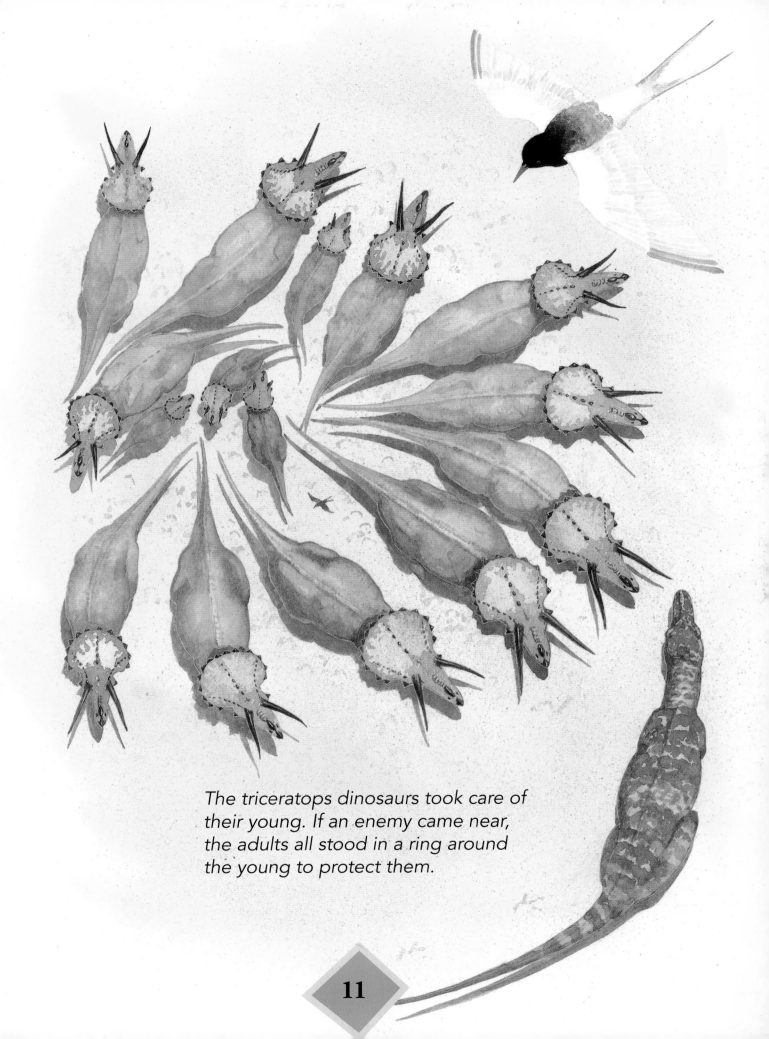

The triceratops dinosaurs took care of their young. If an enemy came near, the adults all stood in a ring around the young to protect them.

Short-frilled dinosaurs

There were other kinds of horned dinosaurs, too. Some had short neck frills. Others had longer ones.

The centrosaurus was a short-frilled dinosaur and was smaller than the triceratops. The long horn on its nose, and the spikes on its neck frill made it look very fierce. The centrosaurus lived in herds and fed on plants.

This is how you say centrosaurus:
cen-tro-sore-us

12

CENTROSAURUS

Group: horned dinosaurs (ceratopians)

Length: 20 feet (6 m)

Lived in: North America

When: Late Cretaceous, 76–74 million years ago

PACHYRHINOSAURUS

Group: horned dinosaurs (ceratopians)

Length: 20 feet (6 m)

Lived in: North America

When: Late Cretaceous, 76–74 million years ago

The pachyrhinosaurus may not have had horns. The skulls have just a thick bony pad on the nose. But the horns might have fallen off!

This is how you say pachyrhinosaurus: pack-ee-rine-o-sore-us

Long-frilled dinosaurs

Another group of horned dinosaurs had very long neck frills. The torosaurus was one of these. It had the largest skull of any land animal ever known.

The dinosaur's head and huge neck frill measured more than 8.2 feet (2.5 m). Its horns and frill made it very difficult to attack.

Some experts think that the torosaurus's neck frill may have been covered with colorful skin.

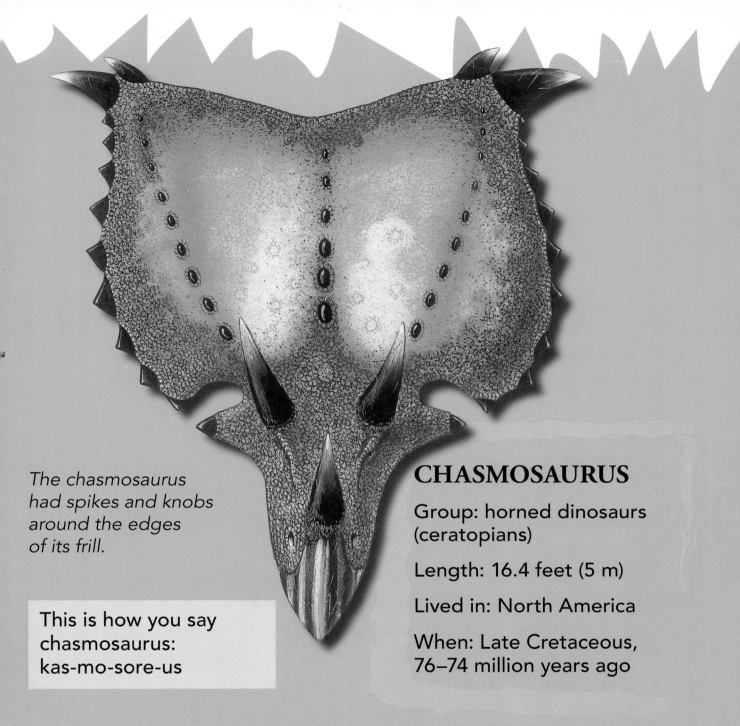

The chasmosaurus had spikes and knobs around the edges of its frill.

CHASMOSAURUS

Group: horned dinosaurs (ceratopians)

Length: 16.4 feet (5 m)

Lived in: North America

When: Late Cretaceous, 76–74 million years ago

This is how you say chasmosaurus: kas-mo-sore-us

TOROSAURUS

Group: horned dinosaurs (ceratopians)

Length: 24.6 feet (7.5 m)

Lived in: North America

When: Late Cretaceous, 70–65 million years ago

This is how you say torosaurus: tor-o-sore-us

Armored dinosaurs: nodosaurs

Armored dinosaurs had built-in suits of armor—flat pieces of bone, set into their skin. Many also had spikes sticking out at the sides of the body.

There were two groups of armored dinosaurs—nodosaurs and ankylosaurs. Nodosaurs were huge, tank-like creatures. Two of the largest were the sauropelta and panoplosaurus.

This is how you say sauropelta: sore-o-pelt-ah

The sauropelta was the biggest nodosaur and was heavier than a rhinoceros.

PANOPLOSAURUS

Group: armored dinosaurs (nodosaurs)

Length: 23 feet (7 m)

Lived in: North America

When: Late Cretaceous, 79–75 million years ago

This is how you say panoplosaurus: pan-o-ploh-sore-us

The panoplosaurus even had plates of bone on its head as extra protection.

SAUROPELTA

Group: armored dinosaurs (nodosaurs)

Length: 21 feet (6.5 m)

Lived in: North America

When: Early Cretaceous, 121–94 million years ago

Armored dinosaurs: ankylosaurs

The ankylosaurs were even more heavily armored than the nodosaurs. They had a tail with a heavy club of bone at its tip to swing against an attacker. Even their eyelids had pieces of bone that came down over them like shutters.

Like all of the ankylosaurs, the saichania ate plants. It could chop big mouthfuls with its sharp beak.

This is how you say saichania:
sy-chan-ee-a

SAICHANIA

Group: armored dinosaurs (ankylosaurs)

Length: 21 feet (6.5 m)

Lived in: Mongolia

When: Late Cretaceous, 80 million years ago

EUOPLOCEPHALUS

Group: armored dinosaurs
(ankylosaurs)

Length: 23 feet (7 m)

Lived in: North America

When: Late Cretaceous,
76–70 million years ago

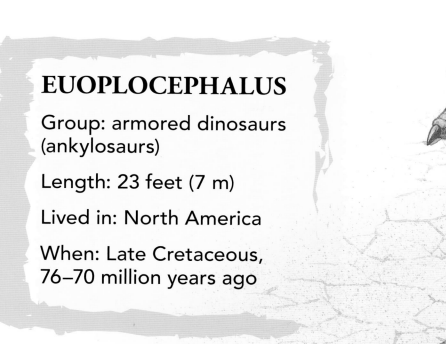

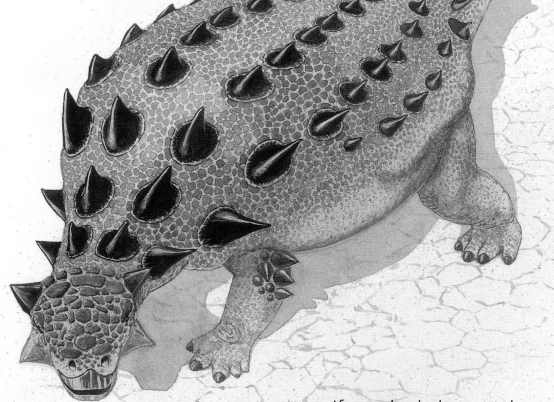

*If attacked, the euoplocephalus
used all its strength to hit an enemy
with its clubbed tail. This heavy
ball of bone could break another
animal's legs.*

This is how you say
euoplocephalus:
you-o-plo-kef-a-lus

Boneheaded dinosaurs

These dinosaurs had amazing dome-shaped skulls made of a thick lump of bone—like a built-in helmet.

Male boneheaded dinosaurs probably fought fierce battles in the breeding season—just as goats do today. Their bony heads would have protected them as they crashed into one another.

This is how you say stegoceras:
ste-goh-ser-as

STEGOCERAS

Group: boneheaded dinosaurs

Length: 7.8 feet (2.4 m)

Lived in: North America

When: Late Cretaceous, 76–74 million years ago

PACHYCEPHALOSAURUS

Group: boneheaded dinosaurs

Length: 26 feet (8 m)

Lived in: North America

When: Late Cretaceous, 76–65 million years ago

The pachycephalosaurus was the biggest boneheaded dinosaur. The dome on its head grew thicker as the dinosaur grew older.

Male stegoceras dinosaurs fought by charging toward each other and crashing head on. They held their tails out behind to balance.

This is how you say pachycephalosaurus: pack-ee-kef-ah-loh-sore-us

Stegosaurs

These dinosaurs are very easy to recognize. All stegosaurs have large, triangular-shaped bony plates along their backs.

The stegosaurus was the biggest of the stegosaurs. Although its body was huge—bigger than an elephant's—it had a tiny head, which was only 16 inches (41 cm) long.

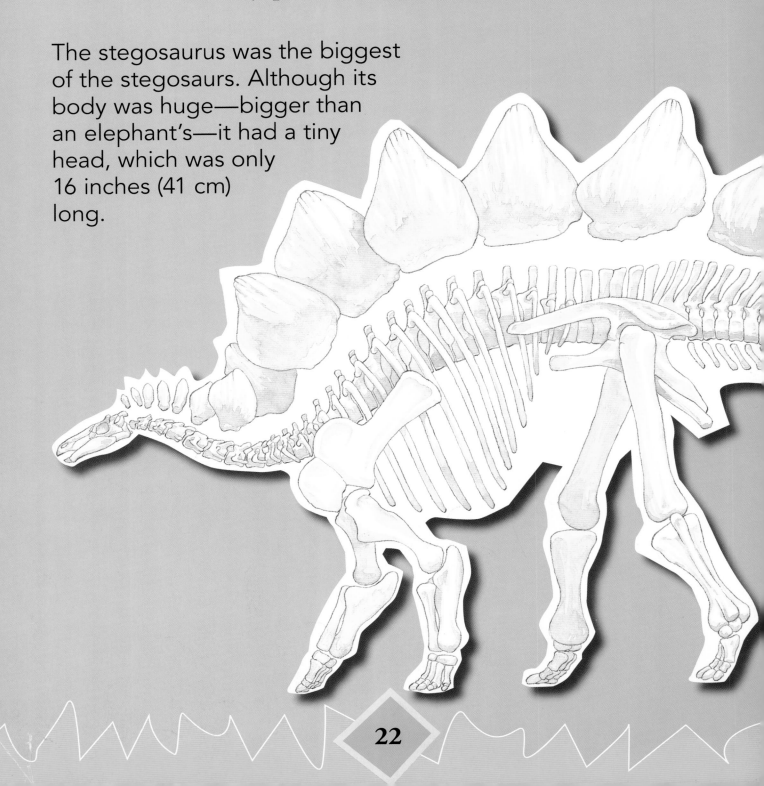

The stegosaurus's big back legs were much longer than its front legs. This made the dinosaur's body slope forward so its mouth was closer to the ground when it was feeding.

STEGOSAURUS

Group: stegosaurs

Length: 30 feet (9 m)

Found in: North America

When: Late Jurassic, 155–144 million years ago

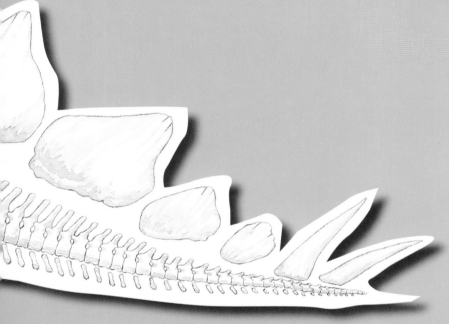

This is how you say stegosaurus: steg-oh-sore-us

The stegosaurus had big, heavy leg bones and a strong backbone to support its great weight. It used the long spikes at the end of its tail to defend itself.

Spiky stegosaurs

The stegosaurus had two rows of large bony plates running from its neck to its tail. The biggest was almost two feet (60 cm) high.

Scientists aren't sure why the stegosaurs had plates, but many think the plates helped the animals warm up or cool down, and made them more difficult to attack.

The lexovisaurus had a sharp spike on each shoulder.

LEXOVISAURUS

Group: stegosaurs

Length: 18 feet (5.5 m)

Lived in: Europe (England and France)

When: Late Jurassic, 170–150 million years ago

This is how you say lexovisaurus: lex-o-vee-sore-us

When the stegosaur was cold, it turned toward the sun. The heat of the sun warmed the blood as it passed through the skin on the plates. When the dinosaur felt too hot, it faced the wind, which cooled the plates and the dinosaur's blood.

This is how you say tuojiangosaurus: too-yan-o-sore-us

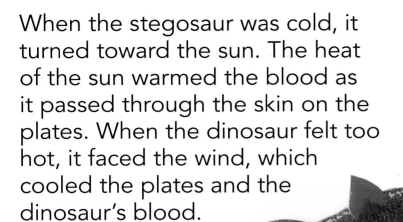

The tuojiangosaurus defended itself with its long spiky tail.

TUOJIANGOSAURUS

Group: stegosaurs

Length: 23 feet (7 m)

Lived in: China

When: Late Jurassic, 157–154 million years ago

A stegosaurus in action

Stegosaurus gobbled up tough leaves
with a sharp, toothless beak at
the front of its mouth.

The dinosaur had small teeth at the
back of its jaws to grind down the
leaves. It moved around on four
legs but could probably stand on its
back legs to reach high leaves.

*The stegosaurus
probably spent
most of the day
feeding, just
as plant-eating
animals do today.*

The stegosaurus was not a fast runner. If danger threatened, it could lash out at an attacker with its heavy, spiked tail.

Dinosaur plants

The triceratops and other horned and armored dinosaurs all ate plants. These big creatures needed a huge amount of food every day, but what kind of plants did they eat?

During the Triassic period, when the first dinosaurs lived, plants looked very different from the ones we see today. There were no flowering plants and no grass. The earth was much drier than it is now, but there were plants such as conifer trees, ferns, horsetails, and palm-like cycads (sy-kads).

cycad

fern

horsetails

28

During the Jurassic period, the weather became wetter and cooler. More and more types of conifers grew and ferns became as tall as trees.

conifer

tree fern

FLOWERING PLANTS

The first plants with flowers and fruits appeared in Cretaceous times. There was more food for plant-eating dinosaurs than ever before and great herds roamed the forests. More and more flowering plants grew, and some earlier plants, such as cycads, became rare.

sycamore

magnolia

Words to know

Armored dinosaurs
Dinosaurs covered with bony spikes and plates to help protect them from enemies. There were two types of armored dinosaurs—ankylosaurs and nodosaurs.

Boneheaded dinosaurs
Dinosaurs with a large bony bump on the skull. The bony bump protected the dinosaur's head in head-butting battles during breeding season. The stegoceras was a boneheaded dinosaur.

Carnivore
An animal, such as the tyrannosaurus, that eats other animals.

Conifer
A type of tree with leaves like little needles. Yews, pines, and monkey puzzle trees are all conifers.

Cycad
Palm-like trees that grew in the days of the dinosaurs. Some cycads still grow today in hot parts of the world.

Fossil
Parts of an animal such as bones and teeth that have been preserved in rock over millions of years.

Herbivore
An animal that eats plants. The triceratops was an herbivore.

Horned dinosaurs
Dinosaurs with big pointed horns and a sheet of bone called a frill at the back of the head. The triceratops was a horned dinosaur.

Neck frill
The sheet of bone at the back of a horned dinosaur's head.

Paleontologist
A scientist who looks for and studies fossils to learn more about the creatures of the past.

Reptile
An animal with a backbone and a dry scaly body. Most reptiles lay eggs. Dinosaurs were reptiles. Today's reptiles include lizards, snakes, and crocodiles.

Tyrannosaur
A type of large, meat-eating dinosaur, such as the tyrannosaurus, that attacked plant-eating dinosaurs.

Index